SPOTLIGHT ON

CLASSICAL STYLE

4 Original Pieces in Classical Style for the Intermediate Pianist

CATHERINE ROLLIN

FOREWORD

The Classical period was an exciting time in the development of keyboard music. Composers were inspired by the recently invented pianoforte and all of the many creative possibilities that this new instrument provided. Also, new forms of music were emerging, particularly the sonata-allegro form that emphasized the development of thematic material and the exploration of harmonic movement. In this collection, it is my goal to explore the sonatina, theme and variations and minuet forms, and to capture the spirit of the Classical period while keeping the technical demands within the range of an intermediate pianist.

CONTENTS

Cover art: Ted Engelbart

Alfred

Sonatina in G

I

Catherine Rollin

* This, and similar measures, should be played staccato and not portato.

* In the Classical period, the exposition was traditionally repeated. In this piece, it is the option of the performer.

37
f
rit.
41
a tempo
45
49
p
mp
53
mf
f

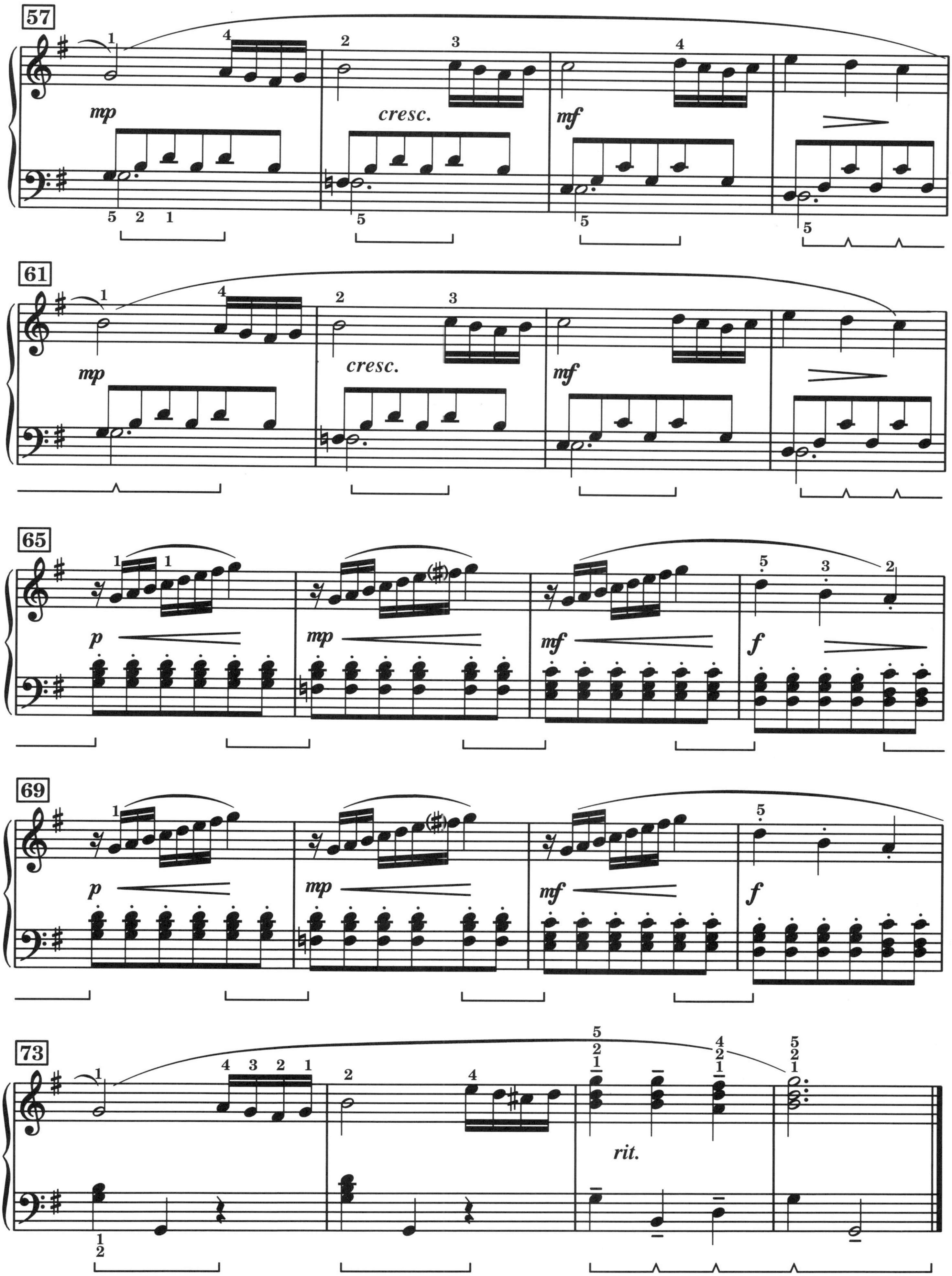
57
mp
cresc.
mf
61
mp
cresc.
mf
65
p
mp
mf
f
69
p
mp
mf
f
73
rit.

II

* It is suggested that finger pedaling be used in the left hand. This is realized as:

13
a tempo
p
17
mf
p
20
mf
p
24
mp
p
rit.

III

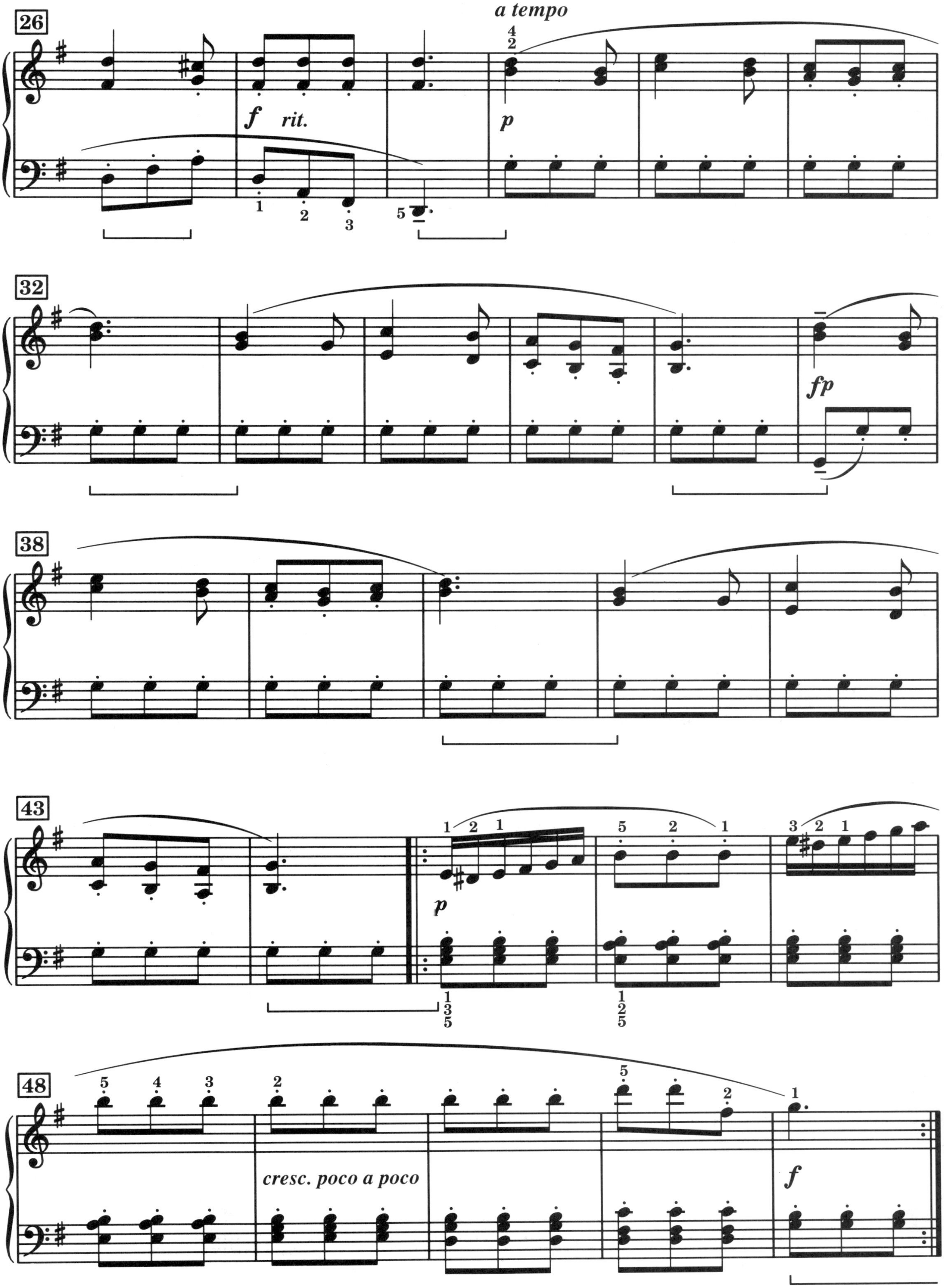
26
a tempo
f rit.
p
32
fp
38
43
p
48
cresc. poco a poco
f

53
rit.
60
a tempo
p
67
fp
74
cresc. poco a poco
80
mf
cresc. poco a poco
f
rit.

Sonatina in C

I

Catherine Rollin

*Measures 17, 19 and other similar measures should be staccato and not portato.

**In the Classical period, the exposition was traditionally repeated. In this piece, it is the option of the performer.

25
p
cresc.
dim.
29
p
cresc. poco a poco
33
f
37
mf
cresc.
41
f

45
mp
cresc.
dim.
49
p
cresc. poco a poco
52
f
dim.
mp
cresc. poco a poco
56
mf
cresc. poco a poco
60
f
rit.

II

Andante

p
poco cresc.
mp
poco cresc.
4
p
poco cresc.
7
mp
poco cresc.
mf
10
mf
poco cresc.

13
mp
poco cresc.
mf
poco cresc.
16
rit.
a tempo
pp
poco cresc.
19
p
poco cresc.
p
poco cresc.
23
mp
poco cresc.
mf
mp
dim. e rit.
p

III

Allegro vivace
p
cresc.
mf
1.
2.
6
dim.
p
dim.
p
12
mp
17
mf
f
dim.
poco a poco
23

29
a tempo
p
cresc.
rit.
mf
p
35
1.
cresc.
mf
41
2.
dim.
p
dim.
mp
47
mf
53
f
mp

58
p
cresc.
rit.
63
a tempo
f
mf
(p on repeat)
68
1.
2.
p
74
p cresc.
mf
cresc.
poco a poco
80
f rit.

Variations on an Original Theme*

Catherine Rollin

*Although it is intended for this piece to be performed in its entirety, it is an option to play selected variations only.

17
mp
22
Variation I
L'istesso tempo
p
27
1.
2.
poco cresc.
mp
32
mf
mp cresc.
36
f
f
f
dim. e rit.

41
a tempo
p
poco cresc.
45
p
Variation 2
Poco piú mosso
poco rit.
mp
49
1.
2.
triplets cont.
mf
simile
54
triplets cont.
mp
mp
59
p
cresc.
fp

63
a tempo
cresc.
fp
cresc.
f
poco rit.
mp
66
simile
Variation 3
Tempo primo
70
mf
p molto legato
74
simile
78
a tempo
poco rit.
mp

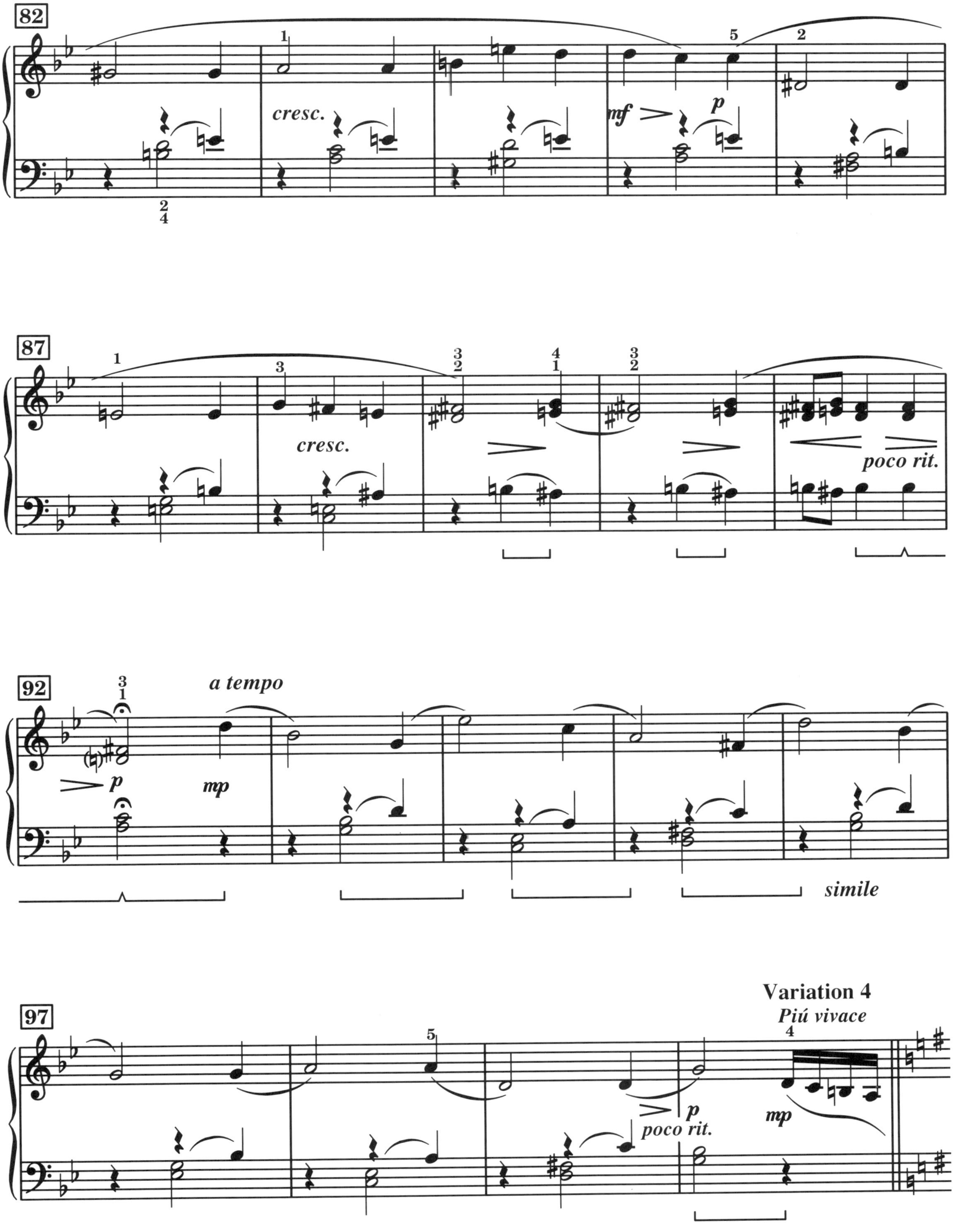
82
cresc.
mf
p
87
cresc.
poco rit.
92
a tempo
p
mp
simile
97
Variation 4
Piú vivace
poco rit.
p
mp

101
104
1.
2.
mf
mp
107
cresc.
mp
cresc.
110
mp
cresc.
113
f

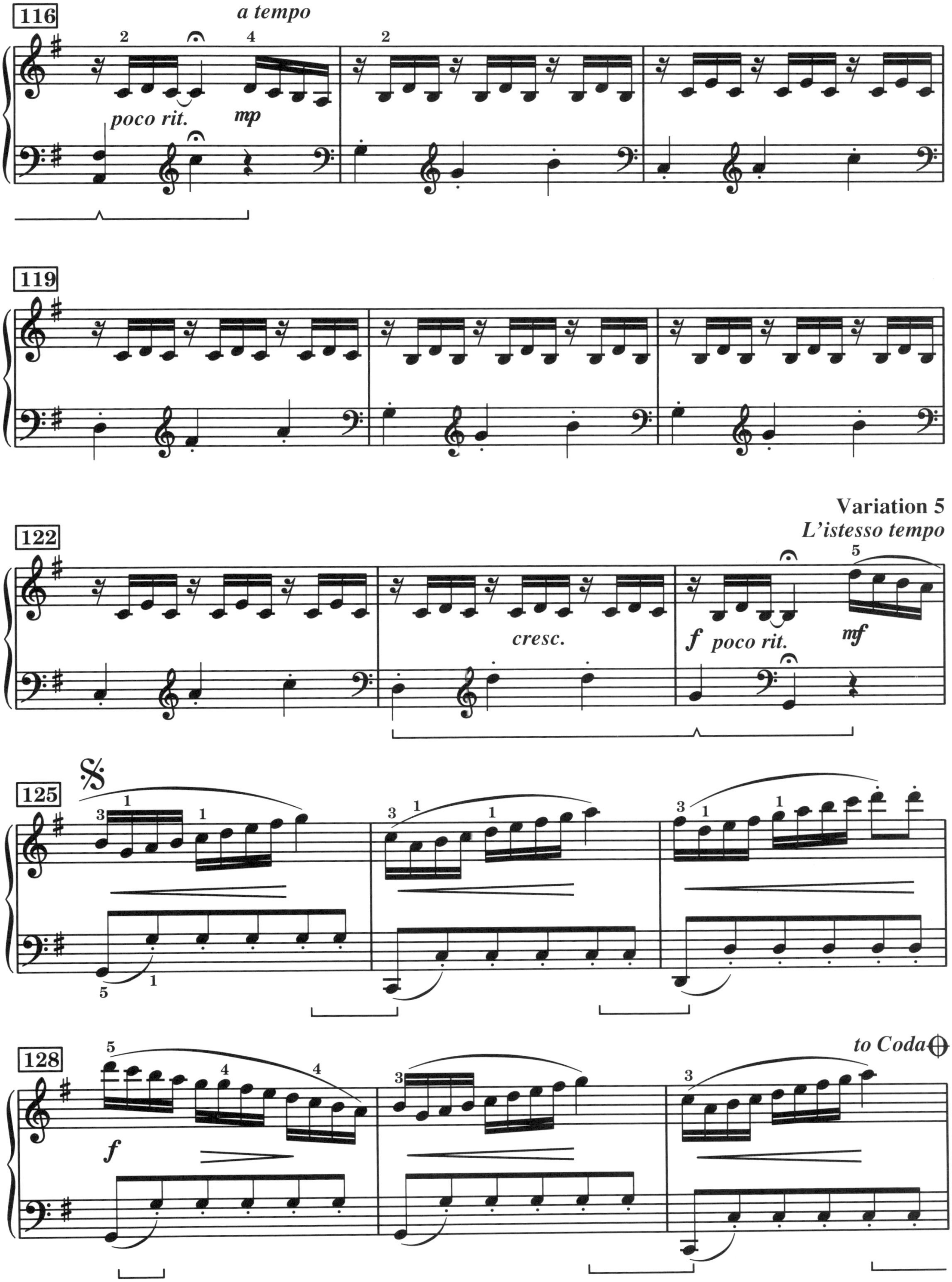
116
a tempo
poco rit.
mp
119
Variation 5
L'istesso tempo
122
cresc.
f poco rit.
mf
125
128
to Coda
f

131
mp
135
mp
p
139
a tempo
dim. e poco rit.
cresc.
f
143
D. S. al coda
mf
CODA
rit.
a tempo
mp
molto cresc.
8va
146
loco
f

Classic Minuet

Catherine Rollin

Andante gracioso

Suggestions & Program Notes

The **minuet** was a French country dance in 3/4 meter that was first introduced in the court of Louis XIV in the middle of the 17th century. It then became a standard movement in Baroque suites. The minuet was the only form of these dance suite movements to continue to flourish in the Classical period. The minuet in this collection is to be played with grace and dignity. (pg. 27)

A **sonatina** (piano sonatina) is a work for solo piano that is typically comprised of three movements. The first movement is fairly fast, the second movement is slower, and the last movement is usually quite quick. The outer movements are generally in the same key, which is the overall key of the piece. The middle movement is in a related but contrasting key.

The two sonatinas in this collection adhere to these characteristics. The first movement of both sonatinas are in a sonata-allegro form. This was the prevailing form for first movements in the Classical period. This form has three major sections: exposition, development and recapitulation. In the exposition, the composer presents the thematic material. Typically, there are two major themes: the first is in the tonic (I) key and the second is in a related key, usually that of the dominant (V). The two themes are also contrasting in character.

The development section employs elements of one or both of the primary themes from the exposition. It develops the initial material through use of dramatic harmonic changes, or other means of exploration. In sonatinas, the development is usually shorter than that of a sonata.

In the recapitulation, the music from the exposition is basically repeated. The most important change, however, is that the second theme is now written in the tonic key. The recapitulation is often followed by a coda which is a concluding section that gives a strong sense of finality to the music. Both of the sonatinas in this collection have a coda. It is suggested that the performer analyze the music and identify the different sections described above. This will help develop an understanding of the structure and will aid in memorization. (pgs. 2–5, 11–13)

The second movements of these sonatinas, and many others, have a songlike quality. They contrast with the first and third movements in key, character and tempo. In *Sonatina in G* the use of finger pedaling is suggested. This is done independently or in conjunction with the damper pedal. The performer holds the first note of each broken chord group in order to give a more sustained, legato sound to the accompanying figure. (See footnote on pg. 6 for the realization of finger pedaling.) (pgs. 6–7, 14–15)

The third movements of both sonatinas are in rondo form. This was a popular form for final movements during the Classical period in sonatas, sonatinas, concertos and symphonies. In this form, the rondo or A theme keeps returning after alternating with contrasting material. In these two rondos the form is ABACA. (pgs. 8–10, 16–18)

Theme and variations was a popular form in the Classical period. It was often used by Mozart, Haydn and Beethoven. In this *Variations on an Original Theme*, as is typical of the Classical period, the thematic material is varied, but the essential harmonies and the ternary structure of the theme are maintained throughout. (pg. 19)